MW01223327

365

CURIOUS

RANDOM

AWESOME

FACTS

? ! WOW! WOW!

AMAZE & ANNOY OTHERS WITH AWESOME CURIOUS KNOWLEDGE

A Year's Worth of Curious Facts

This book belongs to

I have no special talent. I am only passionately curious.

Albert Einstein.

Knowledge has power.

Curiosity is rocket fuel for knowledge!

CURIOSITY is a SUPERPOWER!!

Think! Question! Imagine! GET CURIOUS!
Be inspired! Start a conversation!

Inside this book you will find 365 awesome random curious facts to get you thinking, questioning, and discovering.

When your brain is curious, amazing things happen - learning, memory, questioning and motivation kick into gear. Remembering and learning become easier.

Inside this book you will find facts that will get you curious about things you may never have thought about before.

Every fact is a dose of discovery.

Find out how many people climbed Mt Everest on the busiest day, which famous painting has its own mailbox, the girl with 26 first names, what you call a group of pelicans, the origins of interesting words, what everyday item elephant poo can be turned into, and so much more.

Be prepared for your brain to remember these curious facts and to start thinking and asking questions.
You will want to know more.

Curiosity is rocket fuel for the brain. Get ready for your mind to take off on awesome learning adventures.

Curiosity is rocket fuel for knowledge.

Every fact is a dose of discovery.

The important thing is to not stop questioning. Curiosity has its own reason for existing.

Albert Einstein

1.

The severed head of a sea slug can grow a whole new body.

2.

The moon has moonquakes.

3.

The wood frog can hold its pee for up to 8 months.

4.

It is rare, but a zebra can be born with spots and stripes or just spots instead of stripes.

5.

Lions can see up to 6 times better than humans in the dark.

6.

The Mona Lisa painting in the Louve Museum Paris, has its own mailbox because Mona Lisa receives so many love letters.

7.

Rabbits, squirrels, mice, rats and beavers can't vomit.

8.

Deep in the ocean there is a fish called a Barreleye that has a transparent head and glowing green eyes.

9.

Koalas have fingerprints. Like human prints, each fingerprint has a unique pattern.

10.

A human liver can regenerate in 3 weeks.

11.

The smallest bird in the world is the bee hummingbird which only grows to around 5.7cm (2 & 1/4 inches). Sometimes the tiny bird is mistaken for an insect because it is so small.

12.

The very long word hippopotmonstrosesquippedaliophobia, is the fear of long words.

13.

If all the water on Earth formed a ball, the ball would be 1,384km (860 miles) wide.

14.

It has been mathematically calculated it would take an object 38 minutes and 11 seconds to fall to the centre of the Earth.

15.

An adult human's blood vessels could circle the equator 4 x if they were laid end to end.

16.

The song 'Happy Birthday to You' has been sung on Mars. The robot rover named Curiosity landed on Mars on August 5 2012. One year later, Curiosity was programmed to hum the tune Happy Birthday. The song was recorded and beamed back to Earth. Ten years after landing (2022) Curiosity was still actively sending information back from Mars.

17.

When threatened a sea cucumber can eject its insides out of its rear end to deter predators. Any internal organs lost in the process are usually regenerated by the sea cucumber in a few days.

18.

The average speed of a human walking is 5 km/hr (3-4 mph).

19.

During the Middle Ages in Europe eels were sometimes used as money.

20.

A human can fill around 416 cups of sweat in bed every year.
That's around 98.5 litres or 26 gallons.

21.

Sloths don't fart. Their gut methane is absorbed into their bloodstream instead.

22.

Sloths can hold their breath longer than a dolphin - up to 40 minutes.

23.

Snakes use tongue flicking to collect information in air chemicals to help them detect prey or danger.

24.

Only female mosquito's bite.

25.

It takes more calories to eat a piece of celery than the celery has.

26.

An American dime has 118 ridges around the edge.

27.

The dingo fence in Australia is the longest fence in the world. It is three times as long as The Great Wall of China.

28.

A giraffe's neck makes up almost half of it's overall height.

29.

The barcode for identifying products was invented between 1949-1952. The barcode scanner to read the barcodes did not appear in shops until 1974.

30.

A group of frogs is called an 'army'.
A group of toads is called a 'knot'.

31.

The first tin can to store food was made in 1810. The tin opener was not invented until 40 years later. Before the invention of the opener, cans had to be opened with hammers and chisels.

32.

Perfect pitch is the rare ability to sing or recognise any musical note without another to compare it too. It is estimated 1 in 10,000 people have perfect pitch.

33.

Lion's mane jellyfish are the largest jellyfish in the world. They can weigh up to 1000 kilograms. That's the same weight as an adult male saltwater crocodile.

34.

The smallest ocean on Earth is the
Sea of Marmara which is between the
Black Sea and Mediterranean Sea.

35.

For more than 100 years the Brontosaurus
dinosaur was considered to be a mistake and
had never existed. It was believed the original
Brontosaurus skeleton belonged to a dinosaur
known as an Apotosaurus. However in 2015,
with more dinosaur specimens having been
found scientists concluded there was a
Brontosaurus dinosaur after all.

36.

Brontosaurs means 'thunder lizard', while
Apotosaurus means 'deceptive lizard'.

37.

The animals thought to hear the lowest sounds are elephants and ferrets.

38.

Catchy tunes that get stuck in your head for hours or days are called 'earworms'.

39.

Frogs don't drink water using their mouths, they absorb it using their skin.

40.

The Arctic is mostly sea while the Antarctic is mostly land.

41.

The strongest animal in the world is the dung beetle. Only 10mm long they can lift 1141 times their own weight.

42.

Snails, lobsters, and spiders have blue blood.

43.

The most times a person has been stung by a bee without dying is 2,443.

44.

Fog is made of tiny suspended water droplets. The droplets of water are so small it would take around 7 million droplets to make one tablespoon full of water.

45.

Astronauts lose their sense of smell in space.

46.

The amount of water held in the atmosphere at any one time is about 0.001% of Earth's total water volume.
But it is enough to cover the entire surface of the planet in 2.5cm (1 inch) of water if it condensed and rained.

47.

House flies can travel up to 9.6kms (5.96 miles) in 24 hours.

48.

There are tiny bacteria that lives on human skin and eats the oil it produces.

49.

An aeroplanes 'black box', a device that records conditions and events in flight, is orange in colour.

50.

The ocean contains enough salt to cover all the continents to a depth of nearly 152.4 meters (500ft).

51.

330 million years ago Earth's atmosphere had 1.6 times the oxygen it has today. This oxygen rich atmosphere enabled insects to grow to giant sizes.

52.

The mantis shrimp has the most advanced eyesight on Earth. It can see in ultraviolet, visible, and infrared light.

53.

Alpacas spit when they feel threatened or under attack.

54.

The Empire State Building has its own zip code 10118.

55.

More people live in Bangladesh than is Russia.

56.

The world's largest waterfall is underwater in the Denmark Strait.

57.

The South African Railway once employed a baboon named Jack. He assisted his disabled signalman owner for 8 years, was paid 20 cents a day and never made a single mistake.

58.

The Eiffel Tower is repainted every 7 years.

59.

Catnip can cause cats to be overly excited and anxious but can have the opposite effect on dogs and make them relaxed and less anxious.

60.

The highest toilets in Europe can be found on the French side of Mont Blanc.

61.

Around a fifth of all storks of the world live in Poland.

62.

The largest school in the world is the City Montessori School in Lucknow India. It has over 58,000 students and 4,500 staff.

63.

During World War II, a Great Dane named Juliana living in Britain was awarded the Blue Cross Medal for extinguishing an incendiary bomb by peeing on it.

64.

Hong Kong has more skyscrapers than any other city in the world.

65.

The most climbers ever to reach the summit of Mt Everest in a single day is 234. This occurred on May 19, 2012.

66.

The Nigerian film industry is nicknamed Nollywood. It makes more movies per year than Hollywood.

67.

8.5 litres of water (2.24gallons) can be held in an African elephant's trunk at one time. That's around 36 cups of water.

68.

In three steps a cheetah can go from standing still to sprinting 60km/hr (37.28mph).

69.

160 minutes is the time it took the Titanic to sink.

70.

Hawaii is growing every year and estimated 169,968 square metres due to lava from Kilauea volcano hardening to rock.

71.

In 2014 Gus Andreone was 103 when he became the oldest golfer in the world to achieve a hole in one.

72.

A bee hummingbird can flap its wings 4,800 times per minute.

73.

Sheep have excellent peripheral vision and can see behind themselves without turning their head.

74.

20% of all the fresh water that flows into the world's seas and oceans comes from the Amazon River.

75.

It is estimated 23 million passengers use trains in India every day.

76.

There are around twice as many kangaroos in Australia than there are people.

77.

A walrus can eat as many as 4000 clams and other shellfish in a single feeding session.

78.

Red-bellied piranhas bark to frighten off predators.

79.

A group of piranhas is called a shoal.

80.

A group of narwhals is called a blessing.

81.

Grey whales have the longest migration of any mammal. They can travel 16,000kms (9941miles) each year.

82.

William Shakespeare is credited with inventing over 1700 new words many still in use today, including moonbeam, fairyland, watchdog, bloodsucking, zany, swagger and dwindle.

83.

Eating beetroot can turn your wee pink or red.

84.

Some unusual words invented by
Shakespeare that are not in regular use
today and their meanings include,

Sneap = snub

Foison = abundance

Smilets = attempted half smiles

Immoment = unmomentus

Bubukles = blotches on the face

85.

Crocodiles are continually regrowing teeth.
A crocodile can go through 8000 teeth
in a lifetime.

86.

Ancient Romans used pigeon poo to bleach their hair.

87.

A group of turtles is called a bale.

88.

Blennophobia is the fear of slime.

89.

Ann Pepper was born in 1882 in West Derby Liverpool UK, and was given 26 first names – one for every letter of the alphabet. Her full name was Ann Bertha Cecilia Diana Emily Fanny Gertrude Hypatia Inez Jane Kate Louisa Maud Nora Ophelia Quince Rebecca Starkey Teresa Ulysis Venus Winifred Xenophen Yetty Zeus Pepper.

90.

Rabbits, guinea pigs and baby elephants all eat their own poo.

91.

Saltwater crocodiles are the biggest reptiles living on Earth.

92.

Flamingos pee down their legs as a way of cooling down.

93.

Scientists have discovered herring fish communicate by farting. They send fart bubble messages to each other to help keep the fish group together at night.

94.

Dead skin cells are the main ingredient of household dust.

95.

The Milky Way gets its name from a Greek myth about the goddess Hera who sprayed milk across the sky.

96.

Exploding head syndrome is a condition where during sleep sufferers hear a very loud noise like an explosion. The condition is alarming and exhausting but not dangerous or contagious.

97.

The Pan-American highway is the longest driveable highway in the world, spanning 18 countries and is 48,000 km long (29,825miles).

98.

The biggest antique ever sold and moved is the original London Bridge. It was bought in 1968 and transported to Lake Havasu Arizona USA, where it was reconstructed stone by stone. Reconstruction finished in 1971.

99.

The word atom comes from the Ancient Greek word 'atomos' – which means uncuttable.

100.

The 26th US President Theodore Roosevelt had a pet hyena named Bill. The hyena was a gift from the Ethiopian Emperor. Bill lived at the White House for a time before being relocated to a zoo.

101.

The President Theodore Roosevelt's daughter Alice had a pet snake called Emily Spinach, named by Alice because the snake was green as spinach and as thin as her Aunt Emily.

102.

Cats have fewer toes on their back paws, they have five on the front paws and four on the back.

103.

Alpine bumblebees are capable of flying higher than Mount Everest in simulated lab test conditions.

104.

Ancient Egyptian Queen Cleopatra claimed pickles made her beautiful and kept her healthy.

105.

The British Empire was the most powerful in the 1920's when it controlled 23% of the world's population and nearly a quarter of the Earth's land area.

106.

The temperature of a tennis ball affects how it bounces. Warmer balls bounce higher.

107.

Wimbledon tennis balls are kept at 20 degrees Celsius (68 degrees Fahrenheit)

108.

Venus Cloacina was the Roman goddess of sewers.

109.

Astronaut Eugene Cernan wrote his daughter's initials on the moon in 1974. Cernan was the commander of Apollo 17 and the last crew member to re-enter the lunar module when they were returning to Earth. Just before he left, he wrote his daughters initials 'TDC' on the moon's surface and they are still there today in the lunar dust.

110.

Vikings liked to gift brides kittens as gifts. It was believed the goddess Freya rode a chariot led by cats. Feya was the Viking goddess of love, beauty and fertility.

111.

A medieval cure for a sore throat was to tie a string of worms around your neck. It was thought that when the worms died your sore throat would disappear.

112.

By the time you are six your brain is already 90-95% adult size.

113.

The Night of the Radishes is an annual event held on December 23 in Oaxaca Mexico, dedicated to the carving of oversized radishes and the introduction of radishes to Mexico.

114.

Snowflakes have six sides but are each unique as their shape evolves in the air and no two journeys to the ground are the same.

115.

Australia has the only herd of wild one humped camels in the world.

116.

Saudi Arabia imports camels from Australia.

117.

The world record for skipping a stone on water is 88 skips.

118.

Flies don't have teeth. They have a long tongue that sucks food like a straw.

119.

When a house fly lands on your lunch it vomits on your food. Acids in the vomit dissolve on the food so the fly can suck it up.

120.

Dolphins sleep with one eye open.

121.

In Ancient Greece and Rome spiders' webs were used as bandages because they were thought to be antifungal and have natural antiseptic properties.

122.

The male Amazon River dolphin also known as boto can be pink in colour.

123.

Most woolly mammoths died around 10,500 years ago at the end of the ice age, but a small group survived on Siberia's isolated Wrangle Island until around 4000 years ago.

124.

The world's oldest recorded joke is a fart joke. It is almost 4000 years old and comes from the Sumerian Civilization.

125.

A leapling is someone born on the 29th of February.
It is estimated there are around 5 million leaplings in the world.

126.

Butterflies don't have bones.
They have a skeleton on the outside of their bodies called an exoskeleton.

127.

Some words we use today that come from Viking Old Norse language include snort, lump, scrawny and anger.

128.

An adult basilisk lizard can run across water for about 4.5 metres before sinking.

129.

There were 36 trap doors in the arena of the Colosseum in ancient Rome to let lions and tigers into the arena to do battle with gladiators and slaves.

130.

Some scientists estimate there is around 50 million billion tonnes of salt in the sea.

131.

it is estimated if the sea water dried up a layer of salt 200 metres (0.12 miles) thick would be left over Earth.

132.

Parrotfish sleep in a bubble of their own snot to stop parasites nibbling on them.

133.

There are over three trillion trees in the world, which is around 400 trees for every human.

134.

Fireworks were invented in China around 2,000 years ago.

135.

The biggest land crab is the coconut crab. They can grow up to 1 metre (1.09 yards) wide claw to claw.

136.

Christmas crackers were invented by an English sweet maker called Tom Smith over 170 years ago.

137.

The Spice Girls were originally a band called Touch.

138.

Human teeth are the only part of the body that cannot heal themselves.

139.

A tidsoptomist is someone who's often late because they think they have more time than they do.

140.

Nomophobia is a fear of being without your mobile phone.

141.

The Japanese word 'kuchisabishii' means eating when you are not hungry because your mouth is lonely.

142.

A duel between three people is called a truel.

143.

There are 5 countries in the world with a national anthem that has no words – Spain, Bosnia, Kosovo, Herzegovina, San Marino.

144.

M&M's are named after the business men who created them – Forest Mars and Bruce Murrie.

145.

The world's longest walking distance is 22530 kms (14,000 miles). You can walk from Magadan in Russia to Cape Town in South Africa using just bridges and open roads without flying or sailing.

146.

Decidophobia is the fear of making decisions.

147.

Linonophobia is the fear of string.

148.

Hot water makes a different sound to cold water being poured due to energy molecules moving at a faster rate in hot water.

149.

The television was invented two years after sliced bread.

150.

It took the creator of the Rubik's Cube, Eron Rubik one month to solve the cube after creating it. The current world record for solving it is 4.22 seconds.

151.

Clinomania is an excessive desire to stay in bed.

152.

Baked beans are not baked, they are stewed.

153.

Strawberries can also be yellow or white and some can taste like pineapples.

154.

People cannot sneeze in their sleep due to the brain shutting down the reflex.

155.

Tyromancy is the practice of predicting the future with cheese.

156.

A tittynope is a word to describe crumbs, last drops or any small scatterings of something left over.

157.

An ailurophile is a lover of cats.

158.

The scientific term for brain freeze is sphenopalatine ganglioneuralgia.

159.

An agelast is a person who never laughs.

160.

340 million Lego mini figures are produced each year.

161.

There are around 4 billion Lego minifigures in the world.

162.

The largest population of Japanese people outside of Japan is in Brazil.

163.

Lettuce is a member of the sunflower family.

164.

The cute furry bits inside a cat's ear are called 'ear furnishings', they help pick up faint vibrations and keep the ear clean of dirt.

165.

Scarecrows were once known as 'hobidy-boobies'.

166.

Benjamin Franklin wrote an essay in 1781 titled in part -"Fart Proudly".

167.

Underwater rugby is an international sport.

168.

Sun bears are found in Southeast Asia. They sleep during the day and are active at night.

169.

A group of vultures is called a venue or a committee if they are on the ground.

170.

If a bald eagle loses a feather from a wing, another feather will fall from the same area on the other wing so the eagle can stay balanced when it flies.

171.

A pelican's bill can hold up to 13 litres of water.

172.

Hummingbirds are named after the sound their wings make as they move at super-fast speeds.

173.

A group of pelicans is called a scoop.

175.

Hummingbirds are the only bird that can fly backwards.

176.

In the famous painting Mona Lisa, Mona Lisa does not have eyebrows.

177.

The Mona Lisa painting has been attacked multiple times, the most recent being in 2022 when the glass protecting the painting was smeared with cream cake.

178.

The name of every continent ends with the same letter they start with -Asia, Africa, North America, South America, Antarctica, Europe, Oceania.

179.

Bubble wrap was originally invented as a wallpaper.

180.

Tokyo was originally called Edo.

181.

Camels have three eyelids to help protect their eyes from desert sand.

182.

Phobophobia is the fear of having a phobia.

183.

Fire devils are tornadoes made of flames.

184.

The watermelon is the state vegetable of Oklahoma, USA.

185.

Animals that lay eggs don't have belly buttons.

186.

Accismus means pretending to be disinterested in something when you are actually very interested.

187.

Garden snails are nocturnal.

188.

Snails are born with shells. A baby snails first shell is soft and transparent. The more they grow the harder the shell becomes, and the colour of the shell becomes deeper and darker.

189.

Snollygoster is a word to describe an untrustworthy person.

190.

The average life span of a worm is 2 years but they can live as long as 8 years.

191.

Worms are sensitive to light. If they are exposed to light for too long they can become paralysed.

192.

Worms are older than dinosaurs. They have been around for 600 million years.

193.

A group of worms is called a clew.

194.

Early golf balls were small leather sacs filled with feathers known as featheries.

195.

Toe wresting is a competitive sport with an annual toe wrestling competition held in England.

196.

Tug-o-war was an Olympic sport between 1900-1920.

197.

Extreme ironing is an extreme sport where people take ironing boards to remote locations and iron items of clothing.

198.

A group of crows is called a murder.

199.

The record for barefoot camel jumping is 6 camels. Camel jumping is practiced among the Zaraniq tribe of Western Yemen who inhabit the Red Sea coast of the country.

200.

In France there is a place called Y.

201.

The longest living structure on Earth is
The Great Barrier Reef in Australia.

202.

Trees have the longest lifespan of
all organisms.

203.

Lightening hits oak trees more than
any other tree.

204.

Acacia trees in Africa communicate with
each other by emitting gases to alert other
trees to produce toxic tannin to protect
them from hungry animals.

205.

A group of rhinoceroses' is called
a 'crash'.

206.

85% of all plant life on Earth is in the ocean.

206.

Fourteen new species of dancing frogs were
discovered in 2014, raising the current
number of dancing frog species to 24.

207.

Armadillos are good swimmers and can
hold their breath for up to 6 minutes.

208.

It would take around 18 months to walk all the Great Wall of China. It is 8,046 km (5000 miles) long.

209.

In Ancient Egypt the word for cat was pronounced 'mew' or 'meow'.

210.

To answer a Google query 1000 super computers are used to find the answer in 0.2 seconds.

211.

Abibliophobia is the fear of running out of things to read.

212.

In 2019 the average age of the world's population was 30 years.

213.

The only thing Shakespeare left to his wife in his will was the second-best bed in the house and the linen for the bed.

214.

Apples are more closely related to roses than oranges.

215.

There is a town in Denmark called Middlefart.

216.

Emus are the only bird with calf muscles.

217.

The most forged note in the US is the $20.

In the UK it is the £20.

218.

There are 3 teaspoons to a tablespoon and 8 tablespoons to half a cup.

219.

Avocadoes don't ripen on the tree. They start ripening once they are picked.

220.

The elbow is the hardest, sharpest, and strongest point on the human body.

221.

There are 8 tablespoons in a stick of butter.

222.

Queen Elizabeth II holds the record for appearing on more currency than any other person.

223.

Birds cannot live in space as they
they need gravity to swallow.

224.

The Nobel Peace Prize is named after
Alfred Nobel the inventor of dynamite.

225.

A tsunami can travel as fast
as a jet plane.

226.

Lego makes over 300 million tyres a year.

227.

The word Lego comes from the Danish phrase
'leg godt', which means 'play well'.

228.

A basic eight-studded Lego brick can be combined into 915,103,765 different configurations.

229.

The game Twister was originally called 'Pretzel'.

230.

The inventor of Twister also invented the Nerf Ball.

231.

Two words 15 letters long that don't repeat any letters are uncopyrightable and dermatoglyphics.

232.

Apples float because they are 1 quarter air.

233.

The word human comes from the Latin word 'humus' which means 'earth' or 'ground'.

234.

Peanuts are not nuts. They are legumes and are members of the pea family.

235.

The word animal comes from the Latin word 'animalis' meaning 'having breath', 'having soul', or 'living being'.

236.

The first recorded use of OMG was in a 1917 letter to Winston Churchill.

237.

Ladybugs ooze poison from their knees when threatened.

238.

You cannot smell when you are asleep.

239.

Every human has a unique tongue print.

.

240.

Nudiustertain means the day before yesterday.

241.

The English word with the most meanings is 'run', with 646 different definitions.

242.

Goodbye comes from the phrase 'God be with ye'.

243.

The kangaroo and emu cannot walk backwards.

245.

Night butterflies have ears on their wings so they can avoid bats.

244.

TL;DR is short for - too long: didn't read.

245.

Fingernails grow faster than toenails.

246.

Thumb nails grow the slowest and middle fingernails the fastest.

247.

Your nose gets warmer when you lie.

248.

Some male spiders pluck their cobwebs like a guitar to attract female spiders.

249.

The most expensive version of Monopoly cost US$2 million to make. It included a diamond dice and gold and precious stone houses and hotels.

250.

Only male crickets' chirp.

251.

Australia is the only country on Earth without an active volcano.

252.

The term 'winning something hands down', comes from horse racing. A jockey who is far enough ahead can slacken the reins and keep his hands down.

253.

There are around 3500 varieties of cockroaches on the planet.

254.

A wombat takes 14 days to digest its food.

255.

Endangered polar bears in the Artic
are breeding with grizzly bears
creating 'pizzly' bears.

256.

Sperm whales are the loudest animals on
Earth at 230 decibels.

257.

The Pacific Ocean is larger than all
land masses on Earth combined.

258.

The pressure in the deepest part of the ocean is the equivalent to having 50 jumbo jets on top of you.

259.

The shortest complete sentence in English is – 'I am.'

260.

A boffola is a joke met with extremely loud laughter.

261.

There is a church in the Czech Republic that has a chandelier made of human bones.

262.

In New York it is illegal to sell a haunted house without telling the buyer.

263.

On the top of Mt Everest there is cell phone reception.

264.

The world's largest mountain range is under the sea.

265.

More people live in China today than lived on Earth 150 years ago.

266.

Bolts of lightning can shoot out of an erupting volcano.

267.

Dry sand dunes can produce noises that sound like whistling, singing, squeaking and barking.

268.

Palm trees grew at the North Pole about 55 million years ago.

269.

Anteaters can eat more than 30,000 insects in a day.

270.

A camel does not sweat until its body temperature reaches 41 degrees Celsius (106 degrees Fahrenheit).

271.

A garden snail has a top speed
of 0.48km/hr (0.29 mph)

272.

To make 450 grams (one pound) of honey,
a hive of bees must visit around
2 million flowers.

273.

Pet snails have been known to live
for 25 years.

274.

The blob of toothpaste on a
toothbrush is called a nurdle.

275.

Erases were invented around 200 years after pencils. Before that people used damp pieces of bread to rub out mistakes.

276.

Zippers are named after the noise they make.

277.

Listerine mouthwash was first sold as floor cleaner.

278.

Monkeys and rats can laugh.

279.

Yellow coated graphite (lead) pencils were originally yellow because the colour in China was associated with royalty quality and class.

280.

There is a town in the US State of Arizona called Nothing. No one lives in Nothing.

281.

Two Scottish doctors developed the prototype of the chainsaw to assist in dividing cartilage in childbirth and cutting out diseased bone.

282.

The tiny pocket on blue denim jeans was originally for pocket watches.

283.

The most common fracture in the human body is the collarbone.

284.

Croissants originated in Austria in the 13th Century. An Austrian officer brought the pastry to Paris in the late 1830's when he opened a bakery.

285.

Henry Ford, founder of Ford Motor Company in America, was one of the first tycoons to give his employees Saturdays and Sundays off work and introduced the Monday to Friday work week.

286.

Chocolate milk was originally sold as a medicine.

287.

Aluminium can be recycled indefinitely without loss of quality.

288.

In Scotland there is a village called Dull. It is a member of the League of Extraordinary Communities along with Boring, Oregon USA and Bland in NSW Australia.

289.

A group of wombats is called a wisdom.

290.

Around one third of landfill is made up of packaging material.

291.

The brain itself cannot feel pain.

292.

Hallux is another word for big toe.

293.

Bumbleshoot is another word
for umbrella.

294.

Treasure Island author Robert Louis
Stevenson willed his November 13th
birthday to the daughter of a friend who
did not like her own birthday as it was on
Christmas Day.

295.

Finifugal means being afraid
to finish anything.

296.

A whiffler is somebody who walks
in front of you in a crowd.

297.

Greenland is the least populated
country on Earth.

298.

It only took 6 weeks for Charles Dickens
to write 'A Christmas Carol'.

299.

The word nice originally meant 'ignorant' or 'foolish'. It became a more positive meaning word over time.

300.

Dr Seuss was rejected by 27 publishers before a chance meeting with an old school acquaintance led to his first book, On Mulberry Street, being published.

301.

The candy cane was invented in Germany.

302.

Jingle Bells was the first song played in space.

303.

If you gave all the gifts listed in the song Twelve Days of Christmas it would equal 364 presents.

304.

In Japan there is approximately 1 vending machine for every 27 people.

305.

In World War II Italian doctors came up with a fake disease called 'Syndrome K' to help save Jews who had fled to the hospital seeking protection from the Nazis. Patients with Syndrome K were quarantined, and the Nazis believed it to be a deadly, disfiguring and highly contagious disease.

306.

Ravens mate for life.

307.

There are more bacteria in your mouth than here are people in the world.

308.

One in four hazelnuts grown ends up in Nutella.

309.

Bombardier beetles defend themselves by blasting boiling hot acid from their rear ends.

310.

In 2015 the French court made it illegal to name a newborn child Nutella after the popular hazelnut spread.

311.

Bird poo helps keep the Arctic cool by creating gases that form clouds that shade the Arctic from the sun.

312.

A colony of fire ants can form a raft in times of heavy rain and floods and float for weeks until they reach dry land.

313.

According to legend whistling on a ship could bring bad luck as it was thought whistling presented a challenge to the wind.

314.

Carrots originated in Iran and Afghanistan.

315.

There is an old sailing and boating superstition that says it is good luck to step onto a vessel with your right foot, as stepping with your left brings bad luck for the journey ahead.

316.

The only fish that swims upright is the seahorse.

317.

The dwarf seahorse is the slowest fish in the sea. The dwarf seahorse can only swim 1.5 metres or 5 feet per hour.

318.

Hitler, Stalin, and Mussolini have all been nominated for a Nobel Peace Prize.

319.

Dragonfish teeth are stronger than teeth of great white sharks.

320.

When singing in a group, choir members heart rates can synchronise and beat in the same rhythm.

321.

The Goliath frog is the world's largest frog. It can grow to weigh as much as a house cat and when stretched out be of similar length to a small dog.

322.

Bamboo is the fastest growing plant
in the world.

323.

Giant sea kelp grows faster than
bamboo. Giant sea kelp however is not
classed as a plant but a marine algae.

324.

Sperm whales have the biggest brains of
any animal on Earth.

325.

An African Elephants trunk has
40,000 muscles.

326.

Sea kelp helps calm stormy waters by creating water drag, helping to protect coastlines from wave dangers and erosion.

327.

Sharks have existed before trees.

328.

Nepal is the only country in the world that does not have a rectangular flag.

329.

The study of flags is called vexillology.

330.

Two counties that have square flags are Switzerland and Vatican City.

331.

Giraffes have blueish purple tongues

332.

Monday is named after the moon.
Sunday is named after the sun.

333.

The Atlantic Ocean is growing 3.81cm (1.5 inches) every year.

334.

Alpine Swift birds can sleep while they fly.

335.

The world's largest seed is the coco-de-mer seed of a palm tree.

336.

Architecture was once an Olympic sport. During the first four decades of the Modern Olympics, 151 medals were awarded for music, painting, sculpture, literature, and architecture.

337.

Hailstones have been known to contain tadpoles and frogs.

338.

The first frisbees were made from pie dishes.

339.

Vampire bats drink the blood of cattle.

340.

Times Square in New York used to be a dirt road intersection called Longacre Square. It was renamed Times Square in 1904.

341.

Julius Caesar had a pet giraffe.

342.

Rats teeth keep growing all
through their life.

343.

It is estimated around
6 billion baguettes are produced
by bakers in France per year.

344.

The Caesar Salad was
invented in Mexico.

345.

In 1830 a child as young as five could
work in a coal mine.

346.

Elephant poo can be used to make paper.
One elephant poo can provide around
115 sheets of A4 paper per day.

347.

Today more than half the people

in the world live in cities.

348.

In Japan people use more paper

for manga than toilet paper.

349.

Today there are around 400 gondolas in

Venice. In the 17th and 18th Centuries it is

estimated there were around 10,000.

350.

A gondola deliberately tilts slightly to one
side to balance the weight
of the gondolier.

351.

Yogurt originated in Turkey.

352.

Oxter is an Old English word for armpit.

353.

The current fastest record for a solo
nonstop sail around the world is
49 days 3 hours 7 minutes 38 seconds.

354.

The current record for the fastest flight around the world is
31 hours 27 minutes and 49 seconds.

355.

Argle-bargle is a term for lots of meaningless talk or writing.

356.

It is estimated there are around 3 million undiscovered shipwrecks in the oceans and seas.

357.

The Statue of Liberty wears a
US size 879 shoe.

358.

The biggest mansion in the world is the
Istana Nurul Iman Palace in Brunei. It has
1788 rooms, a mosque and 257 bathrooms.

359.

It is estimated the Statue of Liberty gets
struck by lightening up to 600 times a year.

360.

The Statue of Liberty can sway up to 7.6 cm
(3 inches) in any direction in strong wind.

361.

Cleopatra was not Egyptian, she was Greek. She was last in a long line of Macedonian Greek kings and queens who ruled Egypt.

362.

The platypus is one of the most curious and unique animals in the world. It has a bill like a duck, a tailed like a beaver, feet like an otter, a body covered in fur, is one of only two egg laying mammals left on the planet (the other is the echidna), is semi aquatic (lives on land and in water), does not have a stomach and in the wild can only be found on the east coast of Australia. The male platypus is also one of the worlds few venomous mammals. When the platypus was first discovered many people thought it was so strange it was a hoax.

363.

There is a short horned lizard species found in southern U.S. and Mexico that can aim and squirt blood from their eyes when threatened to defend themselves.

364.

Aromachology is the study of odours on human behaviour, especially senses and emotions. Those who practice aromachology are called aromachologists.

365.

Scientific studies have found the most loved scent worldwide is vanilla.

CONGRATULATIONS!

365 AWESOME RANDOM CURIOUS KNOWLEDGE AWARD

to

Signed:

Date:

Look out for our other fun filled fact books!

Amaze! Surprise!Entertain! Annoy! Improve creativity! Start conversation!

Find out which country does not have mosquitoes, the number of muscles in a caterpillar, which city has its own ant, there to find the longest staircase in the world and much more!

DISCOVER HOW NUMBER FACT KNOWLEDGE EXPANDS THINKING.

Find out how many Earths could fit inside the sun, the new height of Mount Everest, how many jiffy's in a second, the average speed of a garden snail, how long it would take you to count to a billion and much more!

Don't forget to leave us a review so others can find our books too! Thank you !

Be curious always!
For knowledge will not acquire you:
you must acquire it.

Susie Back

Record your own AWESOME RANDOM CURIOUS FACTS :

Record your own AWESOME RANDOM CURIOUS FACTS :

Record your own AWESOME RANDOM CURIOUS FACTS :

Made in the USA
Las Vegas, NV
03 December 2022

61026340R00056